ART NOUVEAU
— COLORING BOOK —

Long before images of pinup girls became popular in the mid-twentieth century, there were the "Chérettes" of Belle Époque Paris. Named after popular French artist Jules Chéret, who revolutionized the color printing process, these idealized women were displayed in a host of advertising posters throughout the city. Featuring dynamic typography, bright hues, and sinuous lines, these posters became the subject of intense public fascination. Some critics even claimed them to be superior to the paintings exhibited in art museums. And when collectors began to steal them as quickly as they could be pasted up, a new term was coined: *affichomanie*, or "poster mania."

Why did people think these posters were so interesting? To put it simply, they had never seen anything like them before. And they were fun to look at: bold, colorful, and large. They became a vital element of an art style called Art Nouveau, or "New Art," which was highly popular in both Europe and North America from about 1890 to 1914. In its organic elements, Art Nouveau was seen as a reaction to the rapid growth of industrial manufacturing.

This coloring book contains twenty-two line drawings of Art Nouveau posters for you to color. The full-color posters are shown as small pictures on the inside front and back covers. When you color in the line drawings, you can copy the original colors or you can be a trendsetter. We've left a blank page in the back of the book so you can create your very own sensation. And don't forget to sign your work with a flourish!

All posters are copyright of Swann Galleries, Inc. The drawings are based on details of the following:

1. Jules Chéret (French, 1836–1932), *Halle aux Chapeaux*, 1892.
2. Georges Lefèvre (French, 1876–1953), *Galeries Artistiques*, 1900.
3. Privat Livemont (Belgian, 1861–1936), *Cacao Van Houten*, 1897.
4. Théophile-Alexandre Steinlen (Swiss, 1859–1923), *Lait pur Stérilisé*, 1894.
5. W.H.W., *Dunlop Cycles*.
6. Hamner (Herman Richir) (Belgian, 1866–1942), *Delhaize Frères & Cie / Au Bon Marché*, 1896.
7. Jean Auzolle (French, 1862–1942), *Fine Champagne*, 1890.
8. Georges Meunier (Belgian, 1869–1942), *A la Place Clichy / Étrennes*, 1897.
9. Eugène Grasset (Swiss, 1841–1917), *Masson / Chocolat Mexicain*, 1897.
10. Hugo van der Woude (?–1913), *Ausstellung künstlerischer Möbel u. Geräte*, 1898.
11. Privat Livemont (Belgian, 1861–1936), *Untitled*, 1901.
12. Théophile-Alexandre Steinlen (Swiss, 1859–1923), *Compagnie Francaise des Chocolats et des Thés*, 1895.
13. Eugène Grasset (Swiss, 1841–1917), *Untitled (Le Parasol)*, 1900.
14. Jules Chéret (French, 1836–1932), *Palais de Glace*, 1896.
15. Louis J. Rhead (American, b. England, 1858–1926), *The Century Magazine for June*, 1896.
16. Frederick Winthrop Ramsdell (American, 1865–1915), *American Crescent Cycles*, 1899.
17. Will Carqueville (American, 1871–1946), *Lippincott's / October*, 1895.
18. Georges de Feure (French, 1868–1943), *Paris-Almanach*, 1894.
19. Louis J. Rhead (American, b. England, 1858–1926), *[L'Estampe Moderne]*, c. 1897.
20. Louis J. Rhead (American, b. England, 1858–1926), *L. Prang & Co's Holiday Publications*, 1895.
21. Heinrich Lefler (Austrian, 1863–1919), *Auer'a Światło*, c. 1896.
22. Eugène Grasset (Swiss, 1841–1917), *L'Éventail*, 1900.

Pomegranate Communications, Inc.
19018 NE Portal Way, Portland OR 97230
800 227 1428   www.pomegranate.com

Compilation © Swann Galleries, Inc.
Line drawings © Pomegranate Communications, Inc.

Catalog No. CB156

Designed by Carey Hall and Becky Holtzman

Printed in Korea

23 22 21 20 19 18 17 16 15 14   10 9 8 7 6 5 4 3 2 1

Distributed by Pomegranate Europe Ltd.
Unit 1, Heathcote Business Centre, Hurlbutt Road
Warwick, Warwickshire CV34 6TD, UK
[+44] 0 1926 430111
sales@pomeurope.co.uk

This product is in compliance with the Consumer Product Safety Improvement Act of 2008 (CPSIA) and any subsequent amendments thereto. A General Conformity Certificate concerning Pomegranate's compliance with the CPSIA is available on our website at www.pomegranate.com, or by request at 800 227 1428. For additional CPSIA-required tracking details, contact Pomegranate at 800 227 1428.

1. Jules Chéret, *Halle aux Chapeaux*

2. Georges Lefèvre, *Galeries Artistiques*

3. Privat Livemont, *Cacao Van Houten*

4. Théophile-Alexandre Steinlen, *Lait pur Stérilisé*

5. W.H.W., *Dunlop Cycles*

6. Hamner (Herman Richir), *Delhaize Frères & Cie / Au Bon Marché*

7. Jean Auzolle, *Fine Champagne*

8. Georges Meunier, *A la Place Clichy / Étrennes*

9. Eugène Grasset, *Masson / Chocolat Mexicain*

10. Hugo van der Woude, *Ausstellung künstlerischer Möbel u. Geräte*

11. Privat Livemont, *Untitled*

12. Théophile-Alexandre Steinlen, *Compagnie Francaise des Chocolats et des Thés*

13. Eugène Grasset, *Untitled (Le Parasol)*

14. Jules Chéret, *Palais de Glace*

15. Louis J. Rhead, *The Century Magazine for June*

16. Frederick Winthrop Ramsdell, *American Crescent Cycles*

17. Will Carqueville, *Lippincott's / October*

18. Georges de Feure, *Paris-Almanach*

19. Louis J. Rhead, [*L'Estampe Moderne*]

20. Louis J. Rhead, *L. Prang & Co's Holiday Publications*

21. Heinrich Lefler, Auer'a Światło

22. Eugène Grasset, *L'Éventail*

Draw and color your own picture here!